A Sun's Journey

A Mother's Memoir of Learning to Let Go

By: Lakisha L. Tucker

Copyright © 2018

ISBN: 9781732213807

This book is dedicated to the men and women who have served this great country. To parents that are learning to let go in all walks of life. To their families for their support, and lastly to my Sun. Thank you for being my hero.

- Lakisha L. Troxler-Tucker

Sometimes you have to step out of line and tie your shoe but once you're done get back in line. Meaning that sometimes life happens and things don't go your way and you would rather give up, but get yourself back together and get back in the line. Have the courage to make your dreams come true, stop letting fear & feet **(Prov. 4:26-27 NIV)** drive your future.

- Daleeia Troxler-Tucker

This book is dedicated in loving memory of Annie Mae Houpe. Thank you for being the epitome of a grandmother.

- Sunrise, September 13, 1950 - Sunset, June 28, 2018

REFERENCES

Batterson, M., & Batterson, P. (2015). The circle maker: dream big, pray hard, think long. Grand Rapids, MI: Zondervan.

Conners, D. (2017, November 8). Why trees shed their leaves[Blog Post]. Retrieved from http://earthsky.org/earth/why-do-trees-shed-their-leaves

Hawkes, Annie S. (1872, June) New National Baptist Hymnal. Based on Psalm 119:10.

The New National Baptist Hymnal 21st Century Edition (2001), Mega Corporation dba Triad Publications..

Silveestro, R. (2014, September 5). Why Leaves Fall from Trees in Autumn [Blog Post]. Retrieved from http://blog.nwf.org/2014/09/why-leaves-fall-from-trees-in-autumn

Young, W. P., Jacobsen, W., & Cummings, B. (2017). The shack: a novel. Newbury Park, CA: Windblown Media.

Edited by: Angel Thurston
Cover and Interior Design by: Tanya P. Roberts

FORWARD

When God blesses you with the gift of children, no amount of reading, or wise counsel from others can prepare you for that reality. Before my wife and I became parents, I remember hearing other parents talk about how children can change your life, but you will never know what the actual experience, of having children will bring into your life, until you hold them in your arms and welcome them into your life. You can assume your reaction will be one way but the actual journey can present you with thoughts and feelings you may not have expected. Through A Sun's Journey, Kisha, as we call her at United Institutional Baptist Church, she gives us a window into her journey, as a mother who has been a part of her son's journey, from birth toward manhood! Reading this book reminds every parent of our own personal story of raising children, and how each of us has attempted to navigate that space, from having them depend on their parents for everything to watching them try to make their own way in the world. I commend you Kisha, for capturing your journey for all that will read this book!

- Rev. Dr. Johnny R. Freeman

DALEEIA

My mother asked me to write my reaction to my brother joining the Marine Corps. For me, when my brother left it wasn't easy. It wasn't easy because I watched my mother and little sister struggle with the idea or now reality of my brother being gone. I am the middle child so

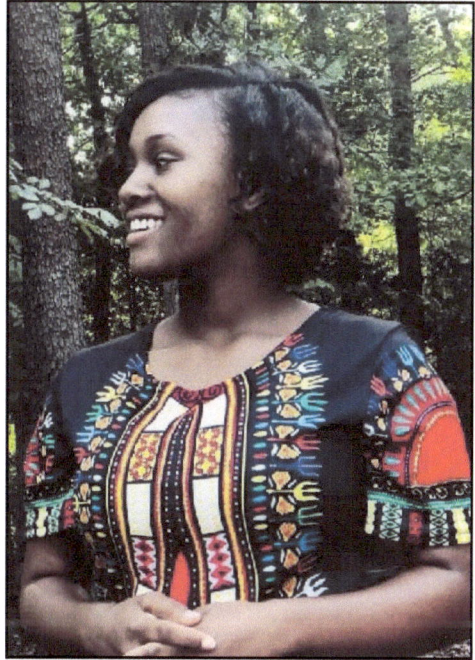

Kiran's Sister: Daleeia Troxler-Tucker

being with my brother was a natural part of life, all I had really known. My brother is seven years older than me, and I am seven years older than our baby sister, Ella.

5,479 days had been spent looking up to him, always there for me. There were times that I would talk to my brother about things that I had not shared with anybody else, not even my mom! When my little sister was born nothing changed. He then had my back and hers'. He showed me that hard work and dedication pays off. I watched him go to work at the grocery store and save his money to buy what he wanted. He worked and went to school. Seeing this made me do better in school both mentally and physically. However, when he left a lot changed. He had been trying to prepare me by saying things like "when I leave your gonna have to do this!" He was talking about his chores that I assumed when he departed. He could knock the dishes out in 20 minutes or so, where it takes me 40 minutes. His idea was to "just get it done." My idea was to delay, delay, delay, until mom forgets what she asks me to do. Now, I use it as a time of peace. I also had to begin taking the dog out and bringing him in, along with feeding him. I realized that my brother was doing more than I ever thought. In school, my grades started to DROP drastically. When he was home, or in the states my grades were always good. When he was away it seemed as if my grades went with him.

Even though people doubted my success, through prayer and preparation, I was able to bring my grades back up. It seemed as if my life was a roller coaster, and I was dangling by a string to keep myself emotionally together.

My brother as you can tell is my everything. In learning to cope and finding ways to support my brother the second year seemed to be easier at times. It became easier to come home and him not be there. I learned to call him in the morning on the way to the bus stop, or in the evening. The times he came home always seemed short, he was

in on Friday, and gone on Sunday. You would think it gets easier, but you just get accustom to it. I love my brother.

If I could say an encouraging word to the siblings or younger family members I would say "keep your head up and don't let sadness take over." I would encourage you to express your feelings openly, and not hold them inside. Nothing is wrong with crying, or missing your family member. The bible verse that keeps me is: *"I can do all things through him that strengthens me."* (**Phil. 4:13** NIV)

Prayerfully yours,
Daleeia Troxler-Tucker

KIRAN

When I decided that I wanted to go into the service I didn't tell my mom. I didn't tell her because I didn't think she could handle it. It wasn't that I didn't think she was strong, I knew she expected me to go to college. She wanted me to

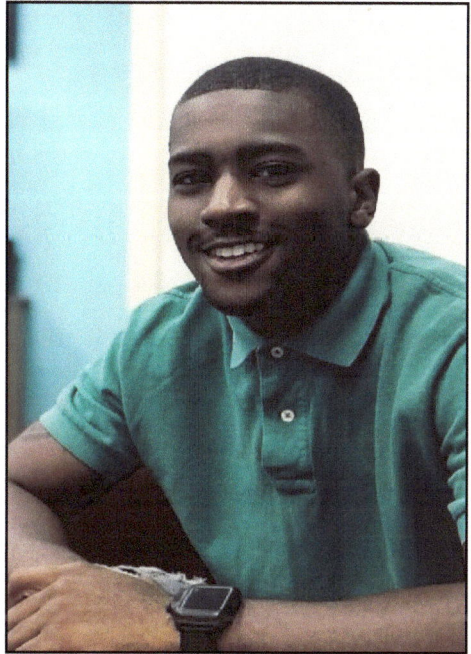

Kiran Morrison

be independent, but not too far from home. There was one occasion when my mom was trying to accept the idea of her "baby" growing up and leaving home that we went to a recruiting station to ask questions. The session became too much for my mom and she took my little sisters and left me there. She did come back, but that's when I knew that me leaving home was going to be harder on her than I originally thought. When she returned she was crying trying to express to me some of her greatest fears.

My mother's love for me was never a question. When I was in high school she was the parent who realized that I hadn't eaten

9

my breakfast and would bring it to me. Yes, I know, she can be extra. I was diagnosed with Attention Deficit Hyperactive Disorder and we had chosen to opt out of medication. Her research showed that if I ate a protein in the morning I could better manage the ADHD. She really was just trying to help. The funny thing was that none of my friends laughed when she did this and my coach just said, "your mama loves you!"

It was that same love that caused others to call me "a Mama's boy!" Initially, I thought that "Mama's boy" meant that I was weak. So, I set out on a mission to prove that I was strong. I decided that I wanted to be a Marine. To prepare myself, I watched videos, talked to others and did research. Once I was equipped with all the knowledge I thought I needed, I talked to the recruiter, and studied for the test. The wheels started turning and the process began.

If I could help someone along the way, I would encourage you to study the service branch you are interested in joining and ask lots of questions. I would encourage you to spend time writing your family, and studying the necessary materials to prepare for the next day while in training. I would also encourage you to enjoy the journey of boot camp. I wouldn't change any portion of that period of time. Know that the daily preparation/obstacles are all necessary for your journey.

I missed my family while I was away, I was reminded not just of their love, but the love of my church family and friends because they all wrote me while I was away. I didn't have time to write everybody back, but I was grateful they thought enough of me to write. I missed my mom telling me what to do, I missed going back and forth with my little sisters laughing and joking. I missed driving my car, talking on my phone, and texting too. But I knew this was short lived, thirteen weeks! "What I learned in boot camp was that I really was a "Mama's boy," and there was nothing wrong with that.

Know that God, has your life framed, and he knows your destiny. You don't have to prove that you are strong. God, has not given you the spirit of fear, but the Lord has given us power. It's up to you to get on board the ship to have a relationship with God. The Marine Corps, has taught me so many lessons; pride, comradery, and allowed me to see places I had never seen before.

The bible verses that keep me are:
(John 15:13, John 9:5, Ps. 23, Phil. 4:13 NIV, 1 Tim. 1:7)

Enjoy your journey, your best days are ahead of you,
Corp. Kiran J. Morrison

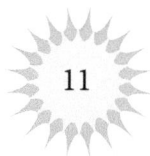

PREFACE

Military Families,

It is a pleasure to be able to share my most intimate feelings about our journey, really his. He reminds me that "I'm not in the Marine Corps, he is!" My Sun, Kiran, has always been affectionately called "SUN," so it is not a typo, that it is spelled SUN and not SON. I remember being pregnant with him, finishing college. There were some difficult days, and the journey became almost unbearable. One afternoon the Oprah show, was on T.V. I remember on the show that day there was a parent that lost her baby, and his name was Kiran. I fell in love with the name, researched it, and decided that was going to be his name. Kiran, means a beam of light, and that's exactly what he has been to me, our family, and others that he has come in contact with.

I pray that this book helps you with the difficult transition. It was one that my family was not ready to embrace, but we did not have a choice. I pray that you will find the courage and strength with the help of Jesus Christ to encourage your recruit, military service men or women. The bible tells us that iron sharpens iron, so one person sharpens another, (**Prov. 27:17 NIV**). So, as you use your time to write letters and

send pictures; make sure your correspondences are positive, uplifting, and encouraging. The rigor of the training is difficult enough don't allow them to worry about home. I encourage you to not only write your recruit, but support others that may not be receiving mail from anyone.

Lastly, thank God for allowing our children to see the day they make their own decisions. They can make decisions that many of their friends could not make because of obstacles, road blocks, or there was another calling on their lives. Keep in mind God is allowing you both this time to develop, to miss one another, and the time to grow closer to him (Jesus). The joy of the Lord is your strength, draw closer to him. We are given the privilege to prepare our (God's children) children for adulthood. When it's time, watch them as they SOAR like eagles.

Enjoy the journey......... it begins now!

A Sun's Journey begins

Blogpost from
https://lakishatucker.wordpress.com/
author/lakishatucker/

My Sun's decision changed our lives forever. As many of you know my sun, their brother made a family altering decision to join the United States Marine Corps (USMC), so as the weeks seem to fly by we were doing all that we could to capture every moment with our future recruit. One evening, I made an executive decision (you know we do that as parents sometimes) that we were going to a movie. The only problem was, none of the movies seemed to be interesting. One movie caught my eye, but I thought the teens/ six-year-old would not be interested, so I previewed the trailer. My initial thoughts were that I was going to justify why we were going to see a Christian movie... and sadly I did. I began to explain to them that if we as Christians did not support Christian movies then why should they continue to make them (they bought it, googled the title and laughed the entire way through the movie).

"Do You Believe?", was the name of the movie I'd selected for the evening. What we didn't know was that we would never be the same after leaving that movie. The movie as described by the author as "A dozen different *souls-all moving in different directions,* all longing for something more. As their lives unexpectedly intersect, they each are about to discover there is power in the Cross of Christ ... even if they don't yet believe it. When a local pastor is shaken to the core by the visible faith of an old street-corner preacher, he is reminded that true belief always requires action. His response ignites a faith-fueled journey that powerfully impacts everyone it touches in ways that only God could orchestrate. This stirring new film from the creators of "God's Not Dead" was in theaters Spring of 2015. More than a movie, it's a question we all must answer in our lifetimes: "Do You Believe?" -Written by Pure Flix Entertainment. The movie was not a disappointment. It was amazing. If you have not seen it and you are looking for a good movie, this is it.

It was after the movie ended that the song We Believe by Newsboys started playing. The Lord took over my spirit as the credits rolled I watched a young man worship, he was not ashamed that others were around. The old song says, "if I couldn't say a word, I'd just wave my hand." That's exactly

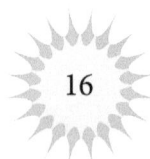

what this young man was doing. What gained my attention all the more was when he moved to the aisle, and began to dance and wave his hands. As I wiped the tears from my eyes I approached his parents thanking them for raising such a free-spirited individual. What shocked me most was when he turned around, he reminded me of a book I read some years ago, "The Shack." He reminded me that God still reigns; He sits high, and looks low.

Zachary introduced himself to me, and I could see that we were different. I'm, an individual that usually tries to contain God, and Zachary is an individual that allows God to just flow through him. What some might say was a coincidence; I believe was orchestrated by God. When I looked at the hat on Zachary's head it said USMC. Spiritually full at this point and continuing to cry, I motion for my family to come back into the theater. When they got close my son calls out ZACK! He responds KIRAN! They knew each other from school.

God knew what I needed that day. I was feeling unsure about my sun leaving, and not being able to talk to him for 90 days, 2,160 hours, 129,600 minutes, 7,776,000 seconds. God knew even though I trusted him, I needed some assurance of what was fastly approaching. Seeing that I could not mail myself to

Parris Island. God used that day to gently prepare me for the upcoming days. It is just like God to show us a yellow brick road when we need to see one, or as some might say, show up and show out! God tells us, *"and Samuel said, Hath the Lord as great delight in burnt offerings and sacrifices, as in obeying the voice of the LORD? Behold, to obey is better than sacrifice, and to hearken than the fat of rams"* (**1 Sam. 15:22 KJV**). In going to see "Do you Believe?" I had been obedient. God reminded me that he would never leave Kiran or forsake us for that matter. If he had kept him from all life's dangers seen and unseen; what made me think that he would not go before him and encamp his angels around this experience and those around him? *"Trust in the Lord with all your heart; and lean not unto thine own understanding. In all thy ways acknowledge him, and he shall direct your path."* (**Prov. 3: 5-6 KJV**)

In the mist of this meeting, Zachary shared that the hat he was wearing belonged to his brother who currently serves our country as a US Marine. He told us that his brother was like the American Sniper, and that he was very proud of him and that his brother's name was Jacob. Their parents shared with our family ways they got through the difficult times.

When the events started to unfold, and Kiran was going through what their mother Bernadine, shared their son went

through, I was thankful for the experience to meet them. I thank God for the opportunity and their willingness to share those intimate details of their life with us.

My Prayer

Dear God,

I pray that we as a nation find that peace that passes all understanding, that peace Dr. King talked about in his I Have a Dream Speech. That we move beyond looking at what church we attend, what neighborhood we live in, how much money we have in the bank, what kind of car we drive, or for that matter what school we send our children too. Not that all of that does not matter but God you said it best. Faith without works is dead. What are we doing to bridge the gap? What are we doing to be our brothers (sisters) keeper? God, you tell us that your word will not return void, and it is my prayer as a believing vessel that we will align ourselves with your standards. God what if, you had not healed the blind man and made him see? What if, you had not cured the woman with the issue of blood, or didn't raise the dead. Would we believe? Would you believe if God had not delivered the Samaritan woman? God, it is my prayer that we come together as a nation and stand on your holy word, and love our neighbor as we love ourselves.   AMEN

I remember something from a book that I am reading, *"The Circle Maker."* The author talks about how we often dream dreams that are small. I knew I needed to learn to dream bigger dreams. It is just like God to use this opportunity and turn it into doing exceedingly and abundantly above all. I am forever grateful. The question is, Do you believe?

https://lakishatucker.wordpress.com/author/lakishatucker/

A very special thank you to Zachary, who lives with Down Syndrome for being so authentic, and allowing God to use him.

A mother's love spans across from heart to heart and breast to breast, thank you to Ms. Bernadine for her comments and support. She mentions that she could remember such an overwhelming feeling of love and pride when they first saw their Marine. I am so excited to be able to stand on the pavement that other mothers and families have stood, waiting to be able to embrace our now recruit soon to be Marine.

To their patient father, thanks for chatting with my husband Eric and sharing encouraging words of hope, faith, and love.

-Lakisha L. Tucker

The Blog Purpose

I decided to start a blog about our journey to the Marine Corps. Kiran, my Sun decided about two or so years ago that he did not want to go to school and that he wanted to serve our country. I could not

We're going all the way

fathom why he wanted to put himself in harms' way. It was not until I realized that God had a greater plan for him than I could ever imagine.

I think about Paul and how he wanted to be a noted preacher, but how God found a much better way to use him. God called a murderer to become an apostle. When I put him in the place of Paul it gave me a since of peace, a calm to the storm. At least to some extent. I thought about how many people Paul was able to witness to while he was imprisoned. That number probably far greater than the number he could have reached in any temple. It is my prayer that he has the spirit of Paul, that he allows God to use him this way.

I remember the first night after he passed the test and that he was going to Military Entrance Processing Station (MEPS). I remember trying to cry silently, then I remember wailing. He came in to ask "what was wrong?", I didn't want to tell him I was afraid of the unknown. Eventually, I was able to say, "I'm afraid that I cannot protect you there, from the unknown." What I really should have said was that "I was not trusting God." It is often much easier to say" I trust God," but when it is your turn to put on the whole armor of God, it doesn't fit, or we are missing bits and pieces of the armor. Am I the only one at times who finds it difficult to digest the decisions of the one's we love, especially our children? I am hoping not. It gives me great comfort to know that I am not the only "mama bear." I am so glad we walk by faith and not by sight.

I was young and now I am old, yet I have never seen the righteous forsaken or their children begging bread. (**Ps. 37:25** NIV)

Trust in the LORD with all your heart and lean not on your own understanding; in all your ways submit to him, and he will direct your path. (**Pro. 3:5** NIV)

ON A PERSONAL NOTE

Thinking about Letting Go, and being Gracefully Broken?
Let me ask you "How do you plan to let go," knowing that God
is using his potter's hands to put you together?

_____

_____

_____

_____

_____

_____

_____

_____

_____

_____

_____

_____

CHAPTER 1

ACCEPTANCE

Weeping may endure for a night,
But Joy comes in the morning.
(Ps. 30:5 (b) NIV)

Are you prepared to birth this new baby? If I may suggest you may want to start thinking about what you want to put in your bag, except this time you are not going to the hospital, but to Graduation.

Can you imagine being pregnant again? Better yet, giving birth again, Get ready, here we go! It must have been his 10th grade year when he decided he was thinking of joining the service. As his mother, I was planning college tours and visits he was not interested at all. We had gone to visit one college and I think (know) that I was more interested than he was. So, when we returned from that trip and I was planning the next, it was at that time he informed me he wanted to be a firefighter. He at this point, never said he didn't want to go to college. There was something in my mind that would not allow me to grasp the concept that he would not be going to

college and earning a college degree it was almost like trying to force two same side magnets together. I'm not sure why it was so important to me, but at the time it was.

I'm not sure if I felt like college was better, or if I was afraid that something would happen to my only sun. It was something about him going to the service that scared me. My thoughts were like, I was walking through a horror movie with the music playing that leads up to a horrific event. Maybe it was the unknown, maybe it was that I didn't trust God enough. Maybe it was the fact that I had limited Gods capabilities. Either way I was afraid, scared, worried or anything else that screamed "Please Don't Go!!"

We signed him up for the firefighter training and I was super excited. Not sure why I was not scared about him being a firefighter. We went to the training, got the papers signed and he was given the equipment. The training began, and he did well. He did so well that during one of the training exercises he was mistaken for a "real" firefighter. The firefighter asked him "what station are you from?". He replied, "I'm in training!" It was amazing to sit and listen to the stories he would tell about what they did each day. That training was short lived and I found the equipment in the trunk of the car, where it stayed

until he turned it in.

He was later employed by a local grocery store where he worked until he graduated from high school. The grocery store provided him with several opportunities to converse with several people that came through his line. Some of the individuals he spoke with were policemen, and state troopers. He developed such a good relationship with them, he knew their stories and what it took for them to get where they were in life. He learned that several of them had military experience that helped them with the training in becoming a policemen or state trooper. I remember going to the District of Columbia, Maryland, Virginia (DMV) area where he spent quite some time talking to the Capital Policemen. Now, the police force had his attention he began to research the requirements. One of the things that frustrated him was the age

Photo By: Brannon Hester

requirement. In order to start the training, you had to be 21. He was only 18!

It was graduation time and I took the opportunity to fill out the form for senior night, because he had not done it. Still hoping that I could talk him into going to college to fill the space between time was still not an option. When his name was called they read his information that I filled out and low and behold HE had changed the "what to do after high school column" from college to military, imagine my surprise. I was smiling and crying inside at the same time. It was almost like looking at a dozen long stem red roses and being stuck by the thorns at the same time. After graduation, he sought employment that would pay him more money. He hoped of being able to get a new car and live on his own. With this particular call center, you had to type a minimum number of words per minute. He was not successful in the first attempt. He has always had determination, it was that determination that led him to download a typing application that would help. With this application, he worked on speed and accuracy. He did just what he set his mind to do, he passed the test, and began working at the call center. He started with training from 4:30 PM until midnight. He successfully completed the training and began working there full-time making "good

money" for a high school graduate.

What I did not know was that during his free time he was taking the (ASVAB) Armed Services Vocational Aptitude Battery practice test which is the assessment the military uses to place service members in their perspective field. Just like the other test he took the practice (ASVAB) Armed Services Vocational Aptitude Battery more than once in hopes of getting a higher score. I will never forget he called me at work and said check your phone! There was a picture with him holding an envelope. He told me he couldn't open the envelop until the recruiter came. He opened it and qualified for a supply job. We were both excited. Our excitement was for different reasons. His because he achieved his goal and mine because he was not on the front line. My thinking was that if he has to go at least he won't be in the line of combat. *(At this point I'm really trying to get there and accept the fact that he is really serious)*

I recall telling him how extremely proud I was of him. I wasn't just proud that he had passed the test, but that he had defeated his own devil. In school years, he struggled with test taking and would become very anxious. I remember that during one of the EOG test he paced the sidewalk the

entire time while waiting on the bus. So, this to us was a big accomplishment! He had finally faced his own fear and won. After he passed the test he signed up for the delayed entry program. We are reminded that the Lord tells us: *"So do not fear, for I am with you; do not be dismayed, for I am your God. I will strengthen you and help you; I will uphold you with my righteous right hand."* (**Isa. 41:10 NIV**). His word also tells us, *"For the Spirit God gave us does not make us timid, but gives us power, love and self-discipline."* (**2 Tim. 1:7 NIV**)

Initial Swearing In

The delayed entry program included him going to work-out with the Marine Corps a few times a week. I began to see the dedication and the pride that was growing inside of him. It was like listening to the ocean as the tide rolls in, getting closer and closer as the sound of the waves get louder and louder. He trained, worked out, did activities with the group and the pride continued to grow.

The next step was to be sworn in, if he was going to do it I wanted to be with him every step of the way. So, we drove to Charlotte to the (MEPS) Military Entrance Processing Station. It was still surreal. We ate at a local sub restaurant after the swearing in ceremony. He continued to train and was given a date for boot camp.

I was paralyzed with fear and found myself weeping all the time. Reality seemed to be setting in. It was like a belt being tightened around my waist cutting off my oxygen, making it difficult to breath. But somewhere, I still thought I had time to change his mind, sad to say it didn't. I was asking God to help me make peace with his decision and if this was to happen to make the way smooth, and if not, show me how to be there for him and how to support him in another role.

There was no stopping what God put into motion. We were given a couple of dates during this time that he might leave. Maybe, just maybe this was the point that it became real! I realized that my baby was no longer a baby, and that he would be leaving soon. He wouldn't just be leaving, but be leaving for the unknown. He would be chartering uncharted waters, not

to mention the fear of the dreaded sand fleas everyone was talking about. As much as I trusted in God and his promise, I was pregnant with fear.

Family Friends Hanging Out

ONE LAST TRIP FAMILY AND FRIENDS...

We decided to take one last trip together as a family in April 2015. We went to Carolina Beach, and for a moment, better yet a weekend we were able to just sit and enjoy one another. There were no worries about what was to come. That weekend came and went so fast (that was just the beginning of how fast they go and come). Before we knew it, we were right back in the preparation stages. This time it was not a drill, we were going live! For the first time in his life I had no control. This time I couldn't tell him "what time to come home," "who to hang out with," or protect him if something happened. I had to completely surrender it all to God because just like seeds falling to the ground it was time for him to be planted, watered, and grow! This was something I could not help him do, he had to do it all on his own.

Sunday Best

Kiran, was an active member of our church. He participated in Sunday School, and was on the men's usher board. I preached my initial sermon April 12, 2015. My first communion was his last time ushering as a civilian. His smile has always been contagious. It was big, bright, and warm. This would just be the beginning of what was to come and how we both would have to learn that even though we were not together we would be in

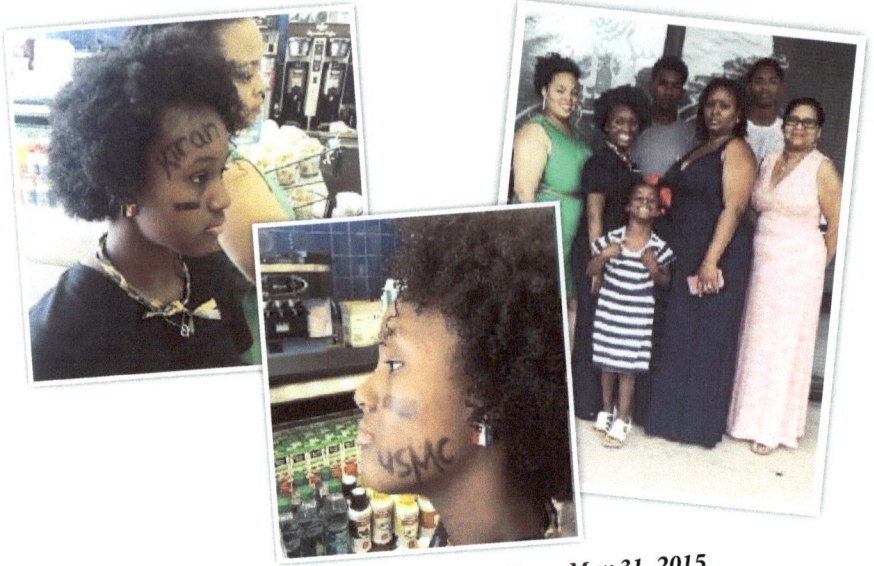

Sister Support On Departure Day - May 31, 2015

the heart of one another. He was always in my heart. Now the test of time would be to discover if our relationship was what we thought it was.

We stopped at Krispy Kreme on the way because at this point I was trying to capture every moment-every second. We arrived at the recruiting station, I promised myself that I would not cry. He was not dying he was going to live his life and I wanted to be a great supporter of that. Besides, I was trying to wear "S" for super mom on my chest.

In the weeks prior to Kiran leaving there was a Bible that the church presented him for graduation 2014. I placed a call to his Godmother requesting bible verses that would encourage him while he was away. This Bible and what he had been taught were the only things that kept us together while he was away. The greatest link was our love for one another. The Bible would serve as a reminder and a little piece of home.

I remember arriving at the (MEP) Military Entrance Processing Station. On June 1, 2015 we could only arrive a few hours early. We arrived in time to eat lunch with him inside the building and it was like we were on a racetrack from the time we arrived. The time seemed to be speeding by. I kept reminding myself that he is NOT DEAD! He's Alive, and alive for a reason. I promised myself I wouldn't cry. While we were waiting I was able to meet other recruits and their parents. There was one family that we seemed to bond with immediately. We exchanged numbers and maintain contact still to this day. Their group was called and the recruits lined up and we circled the room around them. They were sworn in and the families were given minutes to say goodbye. I promised I wouldn't cry at least not in front of him. I did well until we returned the car and I'm sure I cried all the way back home which is about an hour and a half.

God reminded me that he was still large-and-in-charge, while returning the rental car there was a double rainbow that showed up in the sky as his promise to me that he would continue to do what he always has done.

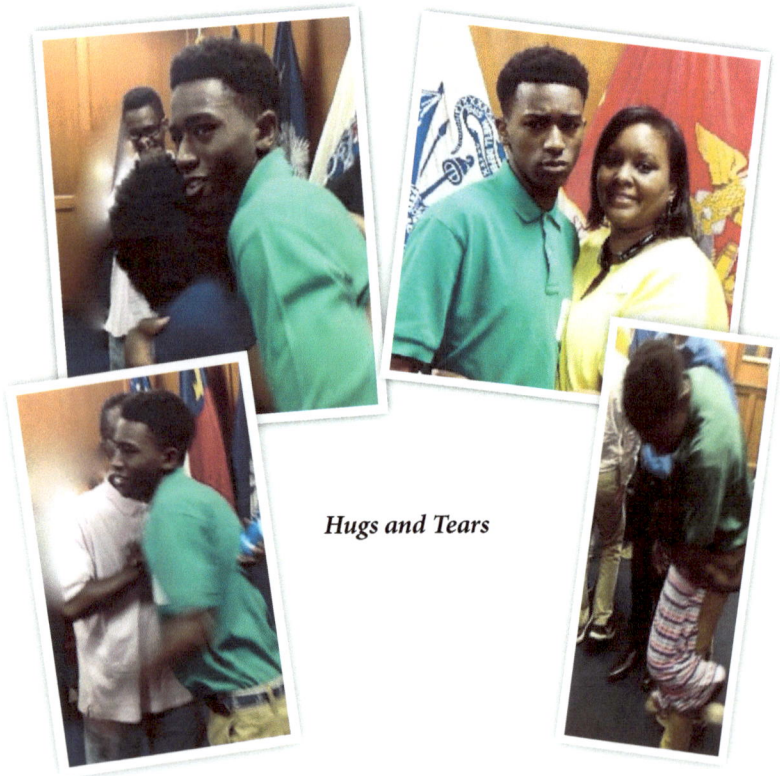

Hugs and Tears

JOURNAL

What were your thoughts when your loved one shared with you they wanted to join the service? How did you come to accept their decision?

_____

_____

_____

_____

_____

_____

_____

_____

_____

_____

_____

_____

_____

_____

5. Trust in the Lord with all your heart and lean not on your own understanding; 6. in all your ways submit to him, and he will make your paths straight. (Prov. 3:5-6 NIV)

CHAPTER 2

LEARNING TO SUPPORT & EMBRACE

TRIMESTER TWO

2 The Lord is my rock, my fortress and my deliverer;
my God is my rock, in whom I take refuge, my shield[a]
and the horn[b] of my salvation, my stronghold. (Ps. 18:2 NIV)

This is recruit Kiran Morrison, I have arrived safely at Parris Island. Please do not send any food or bulky items. I will contact you in seven to ten business days with my new address. (This was my 13 second phone call, where I screamed I love you the entire time he spoke). It was this phone call that ignited my heart to stay strong.

While seeing the double rainbows God reminded me that he had us both covered. *"And God said, "This is the sign of the covenant I am making between me and you and every living creature with you, a covenant for all generations to come: I have set my rainbow in the clouds, and it will be the sign of the covenant between me and the earth. Whenever I bring clouds over the earth and the rainbow appears in the clouds,*

I will remember my covenant between me and you and all living creatures of every kind. Never again will the waters become a flood to destroy all life. Whenever the rainbow appears in the clouds, I will see it and remember the everlasting covenant between God and all living creatures of every kind on the earth." (Gen. 9:12-16 NIV)

The double rainbow we saw after returning to home.

Now it was time to support my sun like never before. Supporting my Sun had never been a problem before, but it was different this time. As a parent, I was typically accustomed to supporting him in things like speeches, football, soccer, basketball, and church events. This type of support looked different because he wasn't physically present. I hadn't dropped him off, wasn't waiting on him in a pick-up line, wasn't waiting on him to call for pick-up, and wasn't waiting for him to call to say he was on his way home.

I had been praying, fasting, and selfishly asking God to keep my Sun with me, although I had been preparing him to leave the nest, when the time came I wasn't ready. I must confess that I was completely wrong. It was during this time that I was trying to still feel connected. I could still smell his smelly shoes, his dirty clothes, and his cologne. I continued to pray about what I could do to remain connected. God, answered me telling me "the recruits are up at 4 am, and if you really want to do something use that time to pray!" So, every morning for 12 weeks my alarm went off at 4 am. It was like I had a routine: I prayed, checked the weather, and went back to sleep when I could.

Kiran's, personality is one that he can get along with almost anyone. When he smiles, he captures the room. When he is in your presence his laughter is contagious. His joy can't be hidden. I am so thankful for the joy he brought to our home. That joy, made it easy when asking his sisters Daleeia, and Ella, to write letters, and draw pictures daily, some days they wrote more than one. Most days I wrote at least two. It was

important for us to keep him in the loop, the loop of our daily activities and to let him know that we had not forgotten about him. I neded him to feel just like he was intertwined with our everyday lives. You might be asking what was there to talk about twice a day? I would begin in the morning telling him about the day we planned. I would end the day writing about what we did and what we were looking forward to the following day. I needed the Marine Corps, not to remove everything he had been taught. We sent pictures, we sent hand drawings, but mostly we sent love. It (love) was in every letter, just like the sand on the beach can't be contained to only the beach. Everywhere you lay your towel or shoes there's sand. I needed him to feel our love stretching from city to city, state to state, grace to grace.

It was the return mail that kept us anticipating everyday like it was a national holiday. The mail in our area ran at that time around at 10:30ish every morning. We would be up dressed and ready to have candy poured into our hands, Kiran's letters!!!!!! The post lady was so nice. She would let us down gently if there was no mail from him. That didn't deter us from using that time to be refueled, for what the next day would bring. You could describe us as steam engines, that couldn't run out of steam. This pretty much sums up the first

three or four weeks. The boot camp calendar is broken up into three portions, I looked at them as trimesters.

In the second phase/trimester where most of us get excited because we can have gender reveal parties and baby showers. It was this phase that we could send protein shakes and bars. It was then that I realized how much 92, of anything cost. Being that there were 92 recruits you had to provide for all of them or they would hold the product until there was enough for everyone, which is only fair. Kiran, would write back and say how much they enjoyed them. The expense became so great that I created a Go Fund me account, and shared the link with the other parents. The response was enormous, they had plenty. Between spending time shopping for protein, the other portion of the day was spent "looking for Waldo." Which is a term used to help you look through the Facebook page and see if you see any pictures of your recruit. Sadly, we never saw our recruit on the site, it was heartbreaking, however it didn't keep us from logging back on and looking again, and again.

The days and nights seemed to get easier until we would go somewhere and order food. It seemed so simple but it was so complex. My routine was to call out each child's name and ask

their order. We were at the window and I began with Sun.... only to recall that he was gone. It was these moments that taught me it is okay to cry, and allow others to see it. I had to realize I was human (you would think I had learned that by now). It was then that I would just break down and cry, and not feel embarrassed or feel the need to explain. It got to the point my girls would say "you miss Kiran?" I honestly found that it made me feel better, it was my catharsis, letting go is not always easy. I found it not only purifying, but refreshing. At one point, I thought I was a weeping willow.

The letters continued back and forth and there were times that the weeks seemed to be speeding up. After processing why, it felt the weeks were speeding up, I realized that I had changed gears. I had gone from reverse to third. I was at the point that I was driven by a higher force, God. I was finally looking toward the future. I was now in fourth gear, planning to pick him up. I spent most of this time online looking for the closest hotel, mapping out the route to the island, and deciding if we would break the trip into more than one day. The other portion of the time I spent ordering the memorabilia items for him online. I ordered so many gifts for him, to remember (like he could forget) the journey. We also enjoyed making the lanterns to display during the crucible.

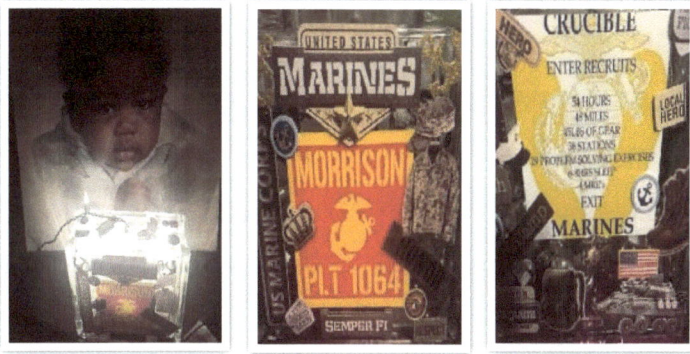

"The Crucible"

The Crucible is a test every recruit must go through to become a Marine. It tests every recruit physically, mentally and morally and is the defining experience of recruit training. The Crucible takes place over 54-hours and includes food and sleep deprivation and over 45 miles of marching.

We decided to break the trip into two days. We stopped halfway rested and ate dinner. We rose early the next morning to begin the final leg or birthing journey of our trip. We planned to arrive Wednesday, because the families were allowed to watch them practice on the parade deck. It had been a long 13 weeks, and if we could get a glimpse of him early that was the plan. Finally, we could see "our Waldo!" As we traveled it was interesting to see the other cars with writing on the windows just like ours that were headed to see their Marines. We were getting more and more excited by the minute, and every passing car!

We finally made it to the island, and there were Marines everywhere. It was not long before we realized that we were standing still and I was being stung by what looked like a colossal red ant. We saw the platoon flag and riffles that we had seen on the internet so many times, however we didn't see the Marines. We took a moment to absorb the surroundings just to see where he spent the last three months. We made our way to the parade deck to see if we could really see him. It was so hot, I'm not sure how we, better yet HE made it. Parris Island is a different kind of hot. As the marines are making their way to the deck, we had succumbed to the heat. My husband, Eric, decided to walk down to see if he could get a closer look. He motioned that he could see him. You can imagine my excitement, I grabbed the camera and ran. The Marines were running and I was praying that being that close I would see him. It was that million-dollar smile and Eric's guidance that assisted me with my first visual. When our eyes met, all I could do was cry. It was as if I was holding my newborn for the first time. While on the parade deck, we saw them

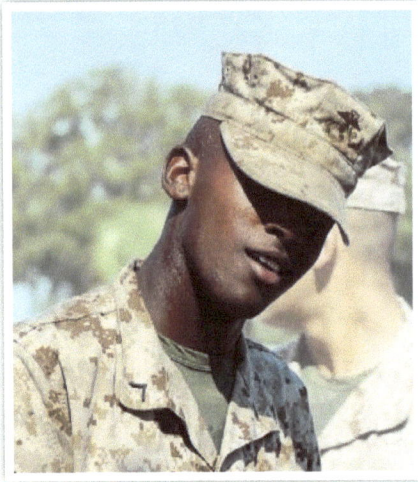

exercise, and practice the drills for the following day. As soon as practice started, it seemed to be over. I thought maybe, just maybe, I could get an up-close glimpse of him. I ran to get into position to get a picture, what I didn't know was that the instructors were going to tell them to run. They all scattered, and I thought I was so close, and not going to see him. It was at this point that I heard him say "MA!" I turned and grabbed the camera and began to snap.

The following day was family day. Family day, was an opportunity for us to spend time with him for a portion of the day. We arrived early with our sign, and we watched them do their morning activities. As we waited, we

Troops Coming In

noticed it was as black as the darkest night. The recruits on the island had on what were called moonlights. Basically, a flashlight on their head. Reflecting on my praying time I had an epiphany. God allowed me to see that during the time I was praying, he was still being guided by the light, the light of the Holy Spirit. One of his favorite bible verses is, *"While I am in the world, I am the light of the world"* (John 9:5 NIV). We saw the lights, they began to sing cadences, and bells began to ring as they had begun the motivational run. After the run, they were instructed to go shower and meet at the next location. While they were showering we were in line to enter the next building. Everything is security, security, security. We lined up and got our space in the building.

They were lined up at the side door and we could see their platoon flag 1064. Their platoon was honor platoon so they were in line first. It was like a garage door was opening, click by click by click, second by second, slowly but surely, we were able to see faces. I began to snap pictures because he had given us his row location. After a few brief words they were ours, well, at least for a few hours. I was finally able to meet the recruits he had written about and HUG my Sun. The week prior to leaving, that Sunday we were finally able to talk with him.

He was able to call using a store phone. He requested one meal for family day, but we had to go to plan "B." We opted for eating outside, but it wasn't long before God reminded us that he was still in control. Sometimes we can do what seems to be a lot of planning and feel like we failed. It's just a reminder that we serve a great God, and he can do whatever he wants to do, Sovereign God. We were forced to pack up our lunch and move to dry grounds, the (PX) Post Exchange. The PX, can be described as a big store with anything you could ever imagine. We were not the only ones who seemed to think that was a good idea, it was full of Marines and their families. This was an opportunity for us to hear the stories and ask lots of questions. We wondered with all the storms how they were kept safe? He, explained that you will hear sirens, and things to alert you to weather conditions on the island.

Kiran, Mom and Grandma's Re-Uniting

It was Friday, time for the moment we had been waiting on, Graduation!! He had so much support, so many wanted to see him, become the Marine he wanted to be. It was a true blessing that both of his grandmothers were able to be present. We lined up again, went through security check and we were seated. There was an over cast, and we were afraid that we would not be able to see graduation on the parade deck. We ask, "God to hold the rain," and he did! This was the moment we had been waiting for, the moment his dreams had come true, and one of the proudest moments of my life. They lined up, marched in, with their Service Charlie uniform, and just like that the ceremony was over. The Marines were dismissed and then there was a great stampede. Everyone was trying to get to their Marine. We hugged, talked and were able to go back to the barracks to gather his things and see where they had been staying and heard some of the stories that took place in Parris Island. We decided not to go straight home but to enjoy South Carolina. We ate at Justine's and hung out that night. We enjoyed the next nine days that he was on leave together in our hometown.

I must admit that even with all the information I read in preparation for his return to civilian world, I was ill prepared. I found that he was a little "stand offish." I was not sure what

happened to the young man that was sent off, but that same young man did not return. He did not talk as much as he did before, and he ate VERY FAST, and did not want to be around large crowds. Who was this MARINE? What I had not taken into consideration, was what he had been through the last 13 weeks, and that not all change is bad. I can remember that I was so worried that I called my pastor, expressing my concern. His response was "give him some time!" That was a valuable lesson for me. Learning again that patience is not my strong suit. Looking back on it, I now realize that I was anxious. Despite the fact that the bible reminds us to be anxious for nothing, my analytical brain was counting the days down until it was time to return him to his next training, School of Infantry, Every Marine is a Rifleman!

Preparing for another goodbye

Before, we knew it the ten day leave was over. We were on the road again. It was awesome to see him take so much pride in his uniform, especially since prior to the USMC, he rarely ironed anything. He checked in and we watched him as far as we could see him and just like that he was gone AGAIN. Like the wind blows so it is told, he held the water jug up and motioned goodbye. This time was not as long, and he could have his phone on the weekends, so we were able to facetime, text, and call. It was the same hustle as before getting to the site on time. Unfortunately, they were doing construction and several people were delayed in arriving. It almost felt like we were watching paint dry. I just knew we were not going to make it, we did, and again we were able to spend the afternoon with him. The Marines were taken to Camp Lejeune where there was a welcome meeting for new families. They shared with the families what the next year would look like as new Marines. Now, we were equipped with the tools needed to support him, we were ready for Marine Family Life!

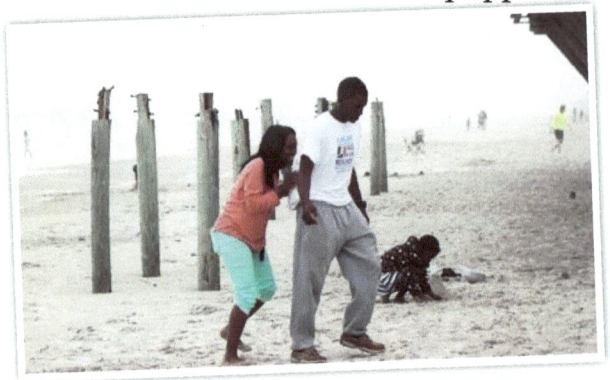

JOURNAL

26 I will give you a new heart and put a new spirit in you; I will remove from you your heart of stone and give you a heart of flesh. 27 And I will put my Spirit in you and move you to follow my decrees and be careful to keep my laws.
(Ezek. 36:26-27 NIV)

_____

_____

_____

_____

_____

_____

_____

_____

_____

_____

_____

_____

_____

_____

_____

_____

_____

_____

_____

_____

_____

_____

3 To everything there is a season, and a time to every purpose under the heaven: 2 A time to be born, and a time to die; a time to plant, and a time to pluck up that which is planted; 3 A time to kill, and a time to heal; a time to break down, and a time to build up; 4 A time to weep, and a time to laugh; a time to mourn, and a time to dance; 5 A time to cast away stones, and a time to gather stones together; a time to embrace, and a time to refrain from embracing; 6 A time to get, and a time to lose; a time to keep, and a time to cast away; 7 A time to rend, and a time to sew; a time to keep silence, and a time to speak; 8 A time to love, and a time to hate; a time of war, and a time of peace.

(Eccl. 3 KJV)

CHAPTER 3
THE LIFE OF A MILITARY FAMILY

And we know that in all things God works for the good of those who love him, who have been called according to his purpose.
(Rom. 8:28 NIV)

The Grand Finale, your holding your new baby and looking into their eyes with pure amazement. The life of a military family really starts the moment your family member decides to join any branch to protect and serve our country. First, let me thank you and your family member for your support and their service. Living the life of a military family means several different things. One of the biggest things I've learned is FAITH. Faith is defined as the substance of things hoped for and the evidence of things not seen. The 91st Psalm is what I always quote to our Marine. The 91st Psalm is what has brought me so much comfort.

"Safety of Abiding in the Presence of God"

91 He who dwells in the secret place of the Most High Shall abide under the shadow of the Almighty. 2 I will say of the Lord, "He is my refuge and my fortress; My God, in Him I will trust." 3 Surely

He shall deliver you from the snare of the fowler[a] And from the perilous pestilence. 4 He shall cover you with His feathers, And under His wings you shall take refuge; His truth shall be your shield and buckler. 5 You shall not be afraid of the terror by night, Nor of the arrow that flies by day, 6 Nor of the pestilence that walks in darkness, Nor of the destruction that lays waste at noonday. 7 A thousand may fall at your side, And ten thousand at your right hand; But it shall not come near you. 8 Only with your eyes shall you look, And see the reward of the wicked. 9 Because you have made the Lord, who is my refuge, Even the Most High, your dwelling place, 10 No evil shall befall you, Nor shall any plague come near your dwelling; 11 For He shall give His angels charge over you, To keep you in all your ways. 12 In their hands they shall bear you up, Lest you dash your foot against a stone. 13 You shall tread upon the lion and the cobra, The young lion and the serpent you shall trample underfoot. 14 "Because he has set his love upon Me, therefore I will deliver him; I will set him on high, because he has known My name. 15 He shall call upon Me, and I will answer him; I will be with him in trouble; I will deliver him and honor him. 16 With long life I will satisfy him, And show him My salvation." **(Ps. 91 NKJV)**

This to me is what I have used as a prayer. I can remember when he was leaving to go to Okinawa one of the last things

I said to him was remember **Psalms 91**. It is hard to put it all into perspective when things seem to be changing and you don't have control of their comings and goings. One of the things that bothered me about coming and going was that we couldn't plan properly. When it comes to deployments they may or may not be home for the holidays, as they were before. Everything is unscheduled, and you have to learn to be resilient. Being resilient may look very different based on where your service member is serving. I found the closer they are the easier it is. The farther away they are, it becomes harder because it takes much more effort on everyone's part to stay connected.

The first holiday he missed was Thanksgiving, then his birthday, and Christmas. We did everything we could to try to get him to come home for Christmas, but he refused. His rational was that he would be home in February. We saved his presents and he tried so many times to get us to tell him what was in the boxes, we didn't! The holidays came and went and we awaited his arrival from Japan, OKI, as he calls it. We had driven down and his fellow Marines signed us in because you have to be sponsored by a Marine to get on base without a pass. We waited on the plane to return to Cherry Point, and the bus to drive them over. We were sitting on pins and needles. He

finally sent a text saying they had arrived. I ask him to let me know which bus he was on and which side so that he was sure to see our sign, and we were sure to see him. We waited outside in the cold against the advice of the USMC. He exited the bus and we screamed!! He saw our sign, and said he couldn't stop and talk. We returned to the barracks and waited again for him to come in to hug him. He was able to grab his things and leave.

Homecoming Welcome
from Okinowa

The second thing we must learn to do is to give up control, and pray like you never have before. *"Only be strong and very courageous; be careful to do [everything] in accordance with the entire law which Moses My servant commanded you; do not turn from it to the right or to the left, so that you may prosper and be successful wherever you go. This Book of the Law shall not depart from your mouth, but you shall read [and meditate on] it day and night, so that you may be careful to do [everything] in accordance with all that is written in it; for then you will make your way prosperous, and then you will be successful." (Joshua 1:7 AMP)*

When you think of strength even when you think you don't have it, when you have to dig deep and find your super parent powers.

Support looks different for different people, we support our Marine, by calling him, texting him, praying for him, and keeping him encouraged. God never ceases to amaze me. In the process of writing this book he was notified that they wanted him to go to Afghanistan. It wasn't long after that that the orders changed and they sent someone else. I was praying the entire time. I'm reminded that the prayers of the righteous availeth much. It was not long after that call, that he was called again and this request was to go over the water. One may ask how can you support him and he is so far away? One might say, he's grown why are you still supporting him? **Deuteronomy 28:4 NIV** helps me to believe that the fruit of my womb is blessed, and the crops of your land and the young of your livestock- the calves of your herds and the lambs of the flocks. I feel that in order for us to care for the seeds that God has given to us that we must prepare them for the unknown.

Supporting your service member maybe sending care packages with their favorite items in them. For us it was decorating a box and filling it with his favorite snacks. We did not just send for him, we also sent enough for those around him. Maybe your support looks different, based on your service member. As civi's (civilians) we may not understand the lingo (language) used by our servicemen or women, but the best way to do anything is to encourage them. I learned when Kiran goes off on a tangent that I have to remind him that I am a civilian and may not understand everything he is saying.

Lastly, pray like you never have before. While writing this book Kiran received orders that he was to spend the remainder of his time in the service (of his active four years) thousands of miles away from home. Initially, as most moms do we try to give words of encouragement to our children. Because I know my Sun, and the fact that he is a home body going that far away is something I did not think he would be interested in doing. WE have always maintained a very close relationship and he had never been more than an hour or so away, an ocean had never separated us before. Going that far away I had to begin to think about how to fill a pool with rain drops, basically one tear drop at a time. When I think about

praying for him, it is almost innate. I pray for those that are around him, the evil doers, those that want to see him fail, and those that want to see him do well. It is my prayer along with Psalm 91, that God would put a fence around him and keep him from any hurt harm or danger. That God would allow him to be able to discern the good and the bad in the people that he may come in contact with. That God would prop him up on the left side when he is weak on the right, and when he is weak on the right that he would prop him up on the left. I pray that God will sustain him through the good and the bad and that the transition would be smooth. That when he gets homesick there would be someone that would give him a tender smile, and show him that they care. That he would be able to call home and hear or see a warm hello. I pray that God would bring him back better than when he left. May this book be a blessing to the many families that sacrifice so much to support their loved ones. May it inspire you to love to the deepest part of your body, and allow you to be the Ezekiel in their lives; to be the wheel in the middle of their wheel, and to speak to their dry bones when they have given all they know to give.

May the love of Jesus fill your life like never before.

JOURNAL

Where there is no vision, the people perish:
but he that keepeth the law, happy is he. (Prov. 29:18 NIV)

_____

_____

_____

_____

_____

_____

_____

_____

_____

_____

_____

_____

_____

5 Trust in the Lord with all your heart and lean not on your own understanding; 6 in all your ways submit to him, and he will make your paths straight.

(Prov. 3:5-6 NIV)

CHAPTER 4

Ella Observes The Season Change

LETTING GO

You will keep in perfect peace those whose minds are steadfast, because they trust in you. (Isa. 26:3 NIV)

As I prepare to let go there are a few things God, has used to remind me that "this is his will." My Sun, was coming home from work late one evening, I heard sirens and the sound of Kiran's car. God, spoke and told me he was in trouble, "get up and get dressed!" I ran grabbed my clothes put them on as I descended the steps, tripping, hopping, almost falling, but still descending the steps. I startled the dog (Sonny Grace, an AKC German Shepherd). Sensing my fear, he barked frantically. I opened the door and was gripped with fear. There was my Sun, sitting in the car, with four police officers surrounding him, and one with his gun pulled, and pointed toward him. Imagine the fear I felt for my young African-American Sun. My heart rate sped up, my breathing was short and rapid and posture tense. The officer was shouting telling me "go back in

the house." I did just as he stated, I went back in the house got my phone, and SonnyGrace, who I affectionaly call "Big Boy." I watched and recorded as they gave him instructions and he followed them.

One of the last policemen to arrive knew him, he said "hey man, you work at the grocery store, right?" He responded "yes." There is always a ram in the bush. Jesus refers to this story in (**Gen. 22:9-13 NIV**).

9 When they reached the place God had told him about, Abraham built an altar there and arranged the wood on it. He bound his son Isaac and laid him on the altar, on top of the wood. 10 Then he reached out his hand and took the knife to slay his son. 11 But the angel of the Lord called out to him from heaven, "Abraham! Abraham!" "Here I am," he replied. 12 "Do not lay a hand on the boy," he said. "Do not do anything to him. Now I know that you fear God, because you have not withheld from me your son, your only son." 13 Abraham looked up and there in a thicket he saw a ram[a] caught by its horns. He went over and took the ram and sacrificed it as a burnt offering instead of his son.

Once, he arrived everyone seemed to calm down. By now the neighbors are peeping out the windows, some standing on the porch and others afraid to help, or comment. Kiran, was given a citation for traveling 85 in a 55. I know what you are thinking, he was speeding right? For the speeders, I am sure you are thinking 85, that's all? This citation delayed the process of entering the Marine Corps. He had to hire an attorney (Attorney Charles Blackmon) and pay the fine. The case was over and he was back on track to entering the Marine Corps. I have heard several sayings that fit this situation "Delayed, but not Denied," "If you take one step, God will take two," "For every setback, there is a setup for God to bless you." As his mother, I was glad it was over and that a traffic ticket didn't kill him physically or mentally.

Traveling to work October 2017, the sun was shining and the wind was blowing, and God began to speak. He said, "do you see the way the trees obey me?" I began to look at the trees sway from left to right, even paying attention to the one or two trees that seem to be dancing to their own music. He quieted my spirit to be in tune to what he was really saying. He said, "even the trees, the winds, and the waves obey me, why are you having a hard time letting go?" He went on to remind me that "to everything there is a season and even

certain trees have to let go of their leaves, why again are you struggling with the decision of letting go, do you trust me?" I was compelled because God and I were having a conversation like I was sending a text message, or on the phone. I replied to him saying "I do trust you, and I am not sure why letting go is so HARD," It is said by the National Wildlife Federation that "evergreens can hang on to their foliage because it is coated in a wax coat that helps to protect against cold, and their cells bear anti-freeze chemicals that ward off winter's worst woes." EarthSky (2016), reports that trees that lose their leaves do so because they are susceptible to being damaged during cold or dry weather. They go further by saying that shedding leaves help trees to conserve water and energy, to allow the tree to reabsorb valuable nutrients from their leaves and store them for later use. Letting go is vital to the trees survival, just as it is to ours!

Letting go HURTS, but it is necessary. October 13, 2017, we made the final journey to Camp Lejeune, for now. Our family loaded up the van to see him off to his new duty station. We picked my Sun up from the base and headed to Wilmington. We were on the road for about five minutes when I heard a loud noise, saw a brown object, and the girls began to say loudly, "I hear something that sounds like air is coming out!" I had not had a flat tire in over 20 years. My thoughts were,

"this cannot be how the last 48 hours will be spent, engulfed in misfortune!" We unloaded all the items in the hatch of the van, and a young gentleman stopped and ask, "do you all need any help?" We declined, but he stopped anyway, another ram in the bush! Mr. Talley, (I don't know his rank) stopped and went right into action. He and my Sun changed the tire, and we headed back into town to try to purchase a new one. We were thinking that we would be there all night, but for Grace, we made a call to Sears, which normally doesn't see customer's after five-thirty in the evening, because they closed at six o'clock. On Friday 13, 2017, they saw us! We were in and out in thirty minutes, and on our way to Wilmington, NC.

We arrived and checked into the hotel. I was feeling that our time had been wasted. I was looking forward to what Saturday would bring. Saturday morning October 14, 2017, started off with me looking for the sunrise over the ocean. It was so cloudy that you could only see the reflection of the rays.

Saturday was amazing, we ate and his father joined us in downtown Wilmington, NC. We decided to try "Breakout." Breakout, is a room filled with different items setup with different themes. We chose "Kidnapped." It was described that we were kidnapped and taken back into time. We had to use different items to make clues, which led you to the next clue. There were two rooms, once you found all the clues in room one, it unlocked the door to room two. We were initially thinking that one hour would not be enough time. We finished in fourty-seven minutes, with thirteen minutes to spare, boy did we feel accomplished.

We finished the day with crab legs, and "she crab soup." As we traveled to the hotel, my mind became the time machine. Counting the time remaining that I had with my Sun. It was nine-thirty and I thought only twelve hours left, 720 minutes.

The day was upon us October 15, 2017. Time for my Sun to make one of the greatest transitions. He was to travel through three time zones in a day. Although, I told myself I would not cry, I could not talk myself into not crying. We arrived at the airport and I immediately went to the restroom, to cry. I managed to get myself together enough to watch my sister help him check-in. The flight attendant thanked him for is service, and helped him select "good seats," on the airplane. We hugged

and said so-long, and he went through the terminal. We waited on the plane to take-off. We were on the inside at first, and he could not see us. We used the light on our cell phone to give him a signal of where we were standing, because he could not see us. The plane began to back out, and we wondered how we could get one last glance. We ran outside and saw the plane sitting, we waved and danced so that he would see us. We circled to pray connecting hearts, and minds. We heard the engine gear up for take-off. We waved one last time. We watched the plane until it completely disappeared. When I could no longer see the plane, I felt as if the breath in my body was tied onto the tale of the plane, and being ripped out. Maybe it was as if, I was superwoman, and my bracelets had been removed. Maybe you can identify better with superman and kryptonite. I let out a cry/yell, which resembled that of a lioness roar.

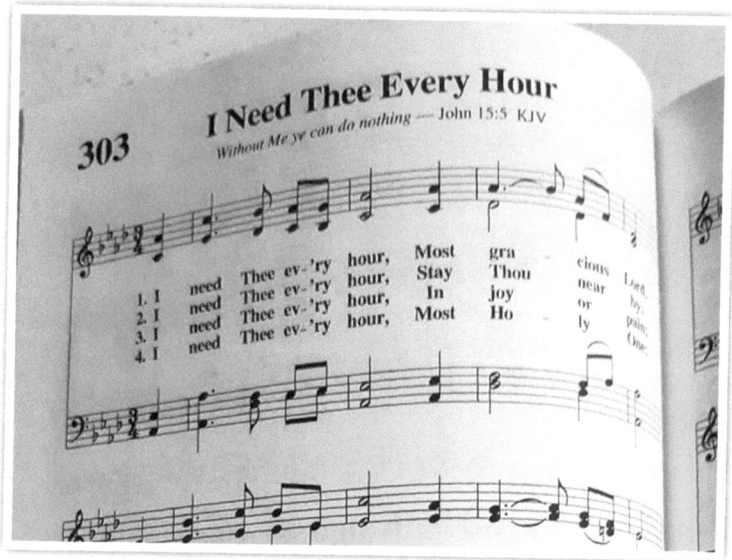

I could hear people talking to me, I told them "I just need a minute!" It was at that moment that I said "God, show me the blessing in this situation." I need thee every hour, most gracious Lord, I need thee, is the hymn that was placed in my spirit. It was a prayer of intercession and petition written by Annie S. Hawkes (New National Baptist Hymnal, June 1872) based on **Psalm 119:10**.

It was then that the bells and whistles began to ring loudly as if I was in the fire department when there was a call for a fire. I pondered the fact that the leaves, before falling they go through cycles of changing colors, just as our family member went through a changing process from birth to adult, for me from "Boy to Man." When I thought about what was changing in my life other than the fact that my Sun, was leaving I thought about faith. Faith that had gotten us through so many difficult situation, Faith that opened doors that no man could open. I hear him saying "Oh ye of little faith." James Cleveland, said it best "where is your faith in God?" As biblically spoken, faith is the substance of things hoped for, and the evidence of things not seen (**Heb. 11:1**).

While listening to Tasha Cobbs Leonard, there was a song that gave my soul peace, "Doves Eyes," a song where some of the lyrics may have come from Misty Edwards. The song simply says "I don't wanna talk about you, like you are not in the room. I wanna look right at you, I wanna sing right to you. Cause, I believe you are listening, I believe that you move at the sound of my voice. So, give me Doves Eyes, Give me undistracted devotion for only you." I wondered just what it meant to have doves eyes? When I think about doves I generally think of them as a sign of peace. They are released at

funerals and seem to give the families a feeling of relief. The Bible makes reference to doves eyes on several accounts:

4 "[a][b]How beautiful you are, my darling, [c]How beautiful you are! Your eyes are like doves behind your veil; Your hair is like a flock of goats That have descended from Mount Gilead. *Solomon's Love Expressed,* (**Sol. 4:1** NIV)

His eyes are like doves by the water streams, washed in milk, mounted like jewels. *(***Sol. 5:12** NIV*)*

I still needed more information about a doves eyes. The more I researched, the more intrigued I became with the binocular vision of doves eyes. It is stated that the binocular vison of a doves eye is sharp and crisp. According to dictionary. com that binocular vision is: vision in which both eyes are used synchronously to produce a single image. Sometimes God will use situations or people to get your attention.

Nest found in the tree at the house. Our reminder that "God Provides"

MY PRAYER

Dear God,

Thank you for always being faithful. Great is your faithfulness, thank you for never giving up on me even when my faith was being tested and I was in doubt. Forgive me Lord Jesus, for not always believing that you would never leave us nor forsake us. Forgive me for thinking that I could ever love him more than you love him. Forgive me for thinking that your Grace would not move from sea to sea. Forgive me for limiting your limitless powers and putting you in a box. Forgive me, for allowing my thoughts not to be your thoughts. Forgive me for being the sinner that I am daily and not always trusting in you. Father God, Forgive me! AMEN

JOURNAL

22 Because of the Lord's great love we are not consumed, for his compassions never fail. 23 They are new every morning; great is your faithfulness. 24 I say to myself, "The Lord is my portion; therefore I will wait for him." 25 The Lord is good to those whose hope is in him, to the one who seeks him; (Lam. 3:22-25 NIV)

Let Your

PRAYERS

Become Your

PRAISE

And

PRAISE

Become Your

PURPOSE

Memory
COLLAGE

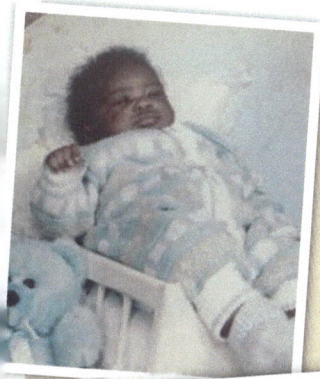

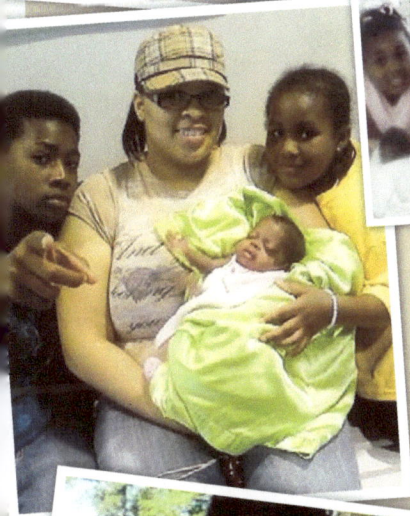

Memory
COLLAGE

Memory
COLLAGE

Memory
COLLAGE

PROUD
FAMILY OF
Kiran Morrison

Memory
COLLAGE

Memory
COLLAGE

Postcard Sayings:
Things you wish you had said...

_____

_____

_____

_____

_____

_____

_____

_____

_____ *Sincerely,*

Postage Paid
Sent to You
With Love

Postcard Sayings:
Things you wish you had done...

_____

_____

_____

_____

_____

_____

_____

_____

_____ *Sincerely,*

Postage Paid
Sent to You
With Love

Postcard Sayings:

Today ...

_____

_____

_____

_____

_____

_____

_____

_____

_____ *Sincerely,*

Postcard Sayings:

We ate at your favorite restaurant and you would have loved...

_____

_____

_____

_____

_____

_____

_____

_____

_____ *Sincerely,*

Postcard Sayings:

You are special to me because...

_____

_____

_____

_____

_____

_____

_____

_____ *Sincerely,*

*Postage Paid
Sent to You
With Love*

Postcard Sayings:

I came across...

_____

_____

_____

_____

_____

_____

_____

_____ *Sincerely,*

*Postage Paid
Sent to You
With Love*

Postcard Sayings:

The path before you is...

_____

_____

_____

_____

_____

_____

_____

_____ *Sincerely,*

Postcard Sayings:

You've come this far...

_____

_____

_____

_____

_____

_____

_____

_____ *Sincerely,*

Postcard Sayings:
The first thing I will say to you is...

_____

_____

_____

_____

_____

_____

_____

_____

_____ *Sincerely,*

Postage Paid
Sent to You
With Love

Postcard Sayings:
Remember when you made me laugh when you...

_____

_____

_____

_____

_____

_____

_____

_____

_____ *Sincerely,*

Postage Paid
Sent to You
With Love

Postcard Sayings:

It seems just yesterday..

_____

_____

_____

_____

_____

_____

_____

_____

_____ *Sincerely,*

Postcard Sayings:

The Lord has brought you through...

_____

_____

_____

_____

_____

_____

_____

_____

_____ *Sincerely,*

Postcard Sayings:

It seems just yesterday..

_____

_____

_____

_____

_____

_____

_____

_____ *Sincerely,*

Postcard Sayings:

The Lord has brought you through...

_____

_____

_____

_____

_____

_____

_____

_____ *Sincerely,*

BIO

Lakisha Tucker is a mother who experienced a breath-taking reality. Her sun spoke the words she feared the most "I want to go into the service, I don't want to go to college!" Lakisha was gripped with fear and she tried to make since of what was happening and why. As she asked herself, "what have I not done that he is not interested in school?" there were several days that she cried trying to "make since" of her Sun's decision. Ill equipped, Lakisha began to research and find out all she could about every branch of service. Her Uncle James, is a Marine, so she knew about that branch, although, her knowledge was still limited.

Lakisha, faced several struggles and uphill battles, while she and her family were trying to get acclimated to military life, transitions, and letting her boy become a man. What she noticed was that there were few to no resources for families that have children leaving home for the military. When having a baby there are books to help with names, and guide you along month by month. But for learning to LET GO... nothing. Nothing makes the process EASY, but support and resources allow the process to become a period of elation. There has been no prouder moment than seeing him stand on that parade deck!!

I encourage you to stay the course, continue to support and love them. Give them their own wings to **SOAR!**

✉ Email us at 50generationsllc@gmail.com

f Like us on facebook.com/50GenerationsLLC/

www.ingramcontent.com/pod-product-compliance
Lightning Source LLC
Chambersburg PA
CBHW051233090426

42740CB00001B/6